THE POWER OF SELF AWARENESS

Ken's Story

A Conversation with
PHILIP BURLEY

Also from Mastery Press:

Mastery Press

Confronting Depression to Stop Suicide
Caring for a Loved One with Dementia
Love Knows No End
The Blue Island
Beyond Titanic—Voyage into Spirit
Heart's Healing
The Spirit World, Where Love Reigns Supreme
The Hum of Heaven
The Wisdom of Saint Germain
The Gift of Mediumship
Awaken the Sleeping Giant
A Legacy of Love, Volume One:
The Return to Mount Shasta and Beyond
To Master Self is to Master Life
A Wanderer in the Spirit Lands

Embracing Your Spiritual Path

THE POWER OF SELF AWARENESS

Ken's Story

A Conversation with
PHILIP BURLEY

Mastery Press

Phoenix, Arizona

Copyright © 2013 by Philip Burley
Published by:

Mastery Press

A division of
Adventures in Mastery (AIM), LLC

All rights reserved. No part of this book may be reproduced or utilized in any form or by any means, electronic or mechanical, including photocopying, recording, or by any information storage or retrieval system, without permission in writing from the publisher. Inquiries should be addressed to:

Mastery Press
P.O. Box 43548
Phoenix, AZ 85080
PB@PhilipBurley.com
(For faster service, please put
Mastery Press in the Subject line)

ISBN: 978-1-883389-20-8

Printed in the United States of America

Philip Burley portrait by Images by Kay
Scottsdale, Arizona

Cover and interior design by 1106 Design
Phoenix, Arizona

DEDICATION

For Ken, the young man whose conversation with me made this booklet possible, and to all those who seek answers that will help them walk their spiritual path peacefully, happily, and successfully to the end.

ACKNOWLEDGMENTS

From early childhood until now, I have been aware of a higher power—an everlasting love that created and guides our lives individually and collectively. To this beloved Being I give the highest acknowledgment for all that has been given, including life—the most precious gift of all!

CONTENTS

Dedication 5
Acknowledgments 7
Introduction 11

PART I:
KEN'S STORY 15
Seeking a Spiritual Foundation 17
Self Discovery Through Meditation 23
Work as a Classroom 33
Embracing Our Life Experience 43
We All Have Truth 49
Saint Germain and Spirit Guides 55
Where To From Here? 59

PART II:
FOLLOW UP CONVERSATION WITH KEN 65
Building a Spiritual Life 67
The Higher Good 69
Growing Through Adversity 71
Easier Is Not Always Better 75
The Second Truth 79

The Power of Self Awareness

A Spiritual Connection............................ 83
The Dating Game..................................... 87
Transforming Energy 93
Maintaining Balance 101

INTRODUCTION

As a full-time professional medium, I am fortunate to have been allowed to intimately share in the lives of thousands who have come to me for more than a quarter of a century for a spiritual reading or intuitive counseling. With their consent I have recorded nearly every spiritual session so I could retain a copy in my files and provide them with a copy for their own use. At the beginning of my work as a medium, those who guide me from the other side asked me to follow this process, and I simply complied.

Further into my work, I could see the universal value of much of the information that comes through me from guides, teachers, and loved ones in the spirit world. Over the years, as I have listened to recorded sessions and learned of their positive effects from many thank-you

The Power of Self Awareness

letters, I realized that they contain a goldmine of spiritual wisdom in multiple expressions—not from me, but from invisible, very real, and most loving spirit beings, including some of the most celebrated spiritual and secular leaders in human history.

In serving as a bridge between this world and the next, I am indeed honored to have been able to bring such deeply personal love and truth to waiting souls on earth. Because their precious questions reflect the longing of all humanity, the answers that come hold significance for many. I am exceedingly grateful that I have been guided to record most of my sessions because they tell the endless story of God's interaction with us through his direct presence and those who come on his behalf. It is my goal, in time, to make most of the material from my records available in some form to the public. In the meantime, I have published a number of books based on my journals and records.

You hold in your hands a book containing the edited transcript of my conversation with Ken[1], a young teacher who came to me for intuitive counseling about his father's death, his

---

[1] Names and some details have been changed to protect the privacy of individuals involved.

Ken's Story

employment, and his future direction. As you would imagine, all identifying information has been excluded.

I share this conversation with you because of the simple yet profound truths that flowed so easily through me in response to the unusual depth of heart and mind of this exceptional young man. As we interacted, I felt removed from ordinary consciousness, as though I were sitting somewhere in Paradise surrounded by august spiritual masters overseeing and guiding our awareness and even our very words. Among my many experiences as a spiritual teacher and medium, this one ranks near the top of those suffused with universal meaning and the personal love and wisdom that comes from the highest levels of spirit. Because of its timeless and universal value, I believe this conversation will speak to you as it has spoken to others who have read it.

It is my good and great pleasure to place this book and its contents in your hands and heart.

—*Philip Burley*

PART I:
KEN'S STORY

SEEKING A SPIRITUAL FOUNDATION

PB: And what would you say is the primary thing you want to talk about?

Ken: I would like to ask you how I can connect more closely with God and with the spirit of my father who died some time ago, as you know. In reading one of your books recently, I was impressed by the consistent spiritual focus in your life and your strong connection with your spirit guides and God. That's what I want—a strong relationship with my own spirituality. When I reflect on it, I feel like I haven't been making my spirituality a high enough priority. To be honest, I go through phases when I pray a lot and others when I don't.

PB: Which book were you reading?

Ken: *The Gift of Mediumship.* I also have *The Wisdom of Saint Germain.*

PB: So if I ask you the question, "What's the foremost thing on your mind?" it's about connecting more closely with God?

Ken: Yes; but I think that ties into other things as well. I'm a little stressed on my new job. I think about my dad a lot, and I have concerns about making the right choices in life. I wonder where I will be in five or ten years. I think a closer relationship with God would help me feel more confident whether I'm at work, thinking about my father, or considering my next steps. But when I try to meditate to develop that closer relationship, I close my eyes and then become kind of lost.

PB: How old are you now?

Ken: I turned twenty-four several months ago.

PB: The most important thing to understand is that life is a process that unfolds in stages, and it's not just a random series of happenings. At any given time, look at what's right in front of you, because that's where God is always working. Whatever your current circumstances at work or

Ken's Story

in other areas of your life, they relate to finding out what you're supposed to learn *now*, in this moment and at this stage of your life. People tend to live without considering their overall direction or a vision for their lives, but if there is one essential key to success, it's knowing your purpose and being consistent in moving toward that purpose.

Soon after we moved to Phoenix from the Philadelphia area, our son took my wife and me to lunch after he graduated from college and started working. He said, "I have observed so many of my peers at school and work living without a sense of purpose, and I'm so grateful to both of you for teaching me that there is a purpose in life, and it's not about just existing." He also said, "Because you taught me self-discipline, I'm much more organized and able to move through life more consciously." This was the highest compliment our son could have paid us.

The central question to ask ourselves is this: "Why am I here, doing what I'm doing?" One good way to gain that awareness is through journaling. I have kept a journal for more than forty years, and writing down where I was, what was happening, and what the life lessons might be from everything that appeared on my path

The Power of Self Awareness

guided me through major life events. My writing has also been a form of prayer, and many pages of my journal are filled with prayer.

I have a question for you, because it's what comes to my mind. Are you a worrier?

Ken: Yes.

PB: Can you tell me what worrying means to you and what you worry about?

Ken: Yes. For me, worrying is about feeling overwhelmed or anxious about something I think I'm not going to get done. I worry about becoming old without accomplishing anything, helping anyone, or doing anything significant. I want to leave my mark on the world somehow, and my greatest worry is that I'm not going to do that.

PB: Your desire to leave a mark on the world, to make a difference, is a noble goal. It's pretty much my own. But I would turn that thought around and impress your consciousness first with the desire to make an indelible mark upon *yourself*—not instead of making a mark upon the world, but in addition to doing that. If you reach out to the world and try to care for other people without first reaching deeply into yourself, you risk losing yourself.

Ken's Story

In having this conversation, you are putting the highest priority where it belongs. Among your most important questions are, "How do I take care of myself? How do I love myself? How do I understand myself? How do I work with myself?" You must answer these questions in order to know how to live your life, because the greatest truth is *within you*, and you can find it only by knowing yourself.

So many people don't know their own potential, and their view of themselves is often critical. Studies have shown that a large percentage of self-talk in people's minds or the words they actually say to themselves under their breath is negative. Does this happen with you?

Ken: Yes. Sometimes I get down on myself.

PB: The best way to deal with it when you find yourself being self-critical is to stop and take the time to listen to what you are saying. It's good to be honest about having made a mistake or taken a wrong turn so you can make a decision to do something differently, but be sure you do this with compassion toward yourself. You can even say, "I love you" as part of your self-talk whenever you become aware that you're having a conversation with yourself. If you don't love yourself, and you just think you should be someone else, somewhere else, and doing something different, you can never be happy. The grass really isn't greener on the other side.

Ken: Right.

PB: It is vitally important to accept yourself exactly as you are and where you are. It's actually an effective spiritual practice to accept what is happening in your life now as what is supposed to happen. This even includes worrying if that's what you're doing. Instead of suppressing worry or coming down on yourself about it, just observe it. The more you step back and look at it objectively, the less you'll worry. Your worry will go away because much of it is coming from your mind and not your soul or spirit.

SELF DISCOVERY THROUGH MEDITATION

PB: When you can look at your life without attachment to what's happening, you'll find greater peace. When we lose objectivity and believe the stories the mind is telling us, we get caught up in our worry and feel anxious. You are not your mind, your emotions, or your thoughts, and you already know that, don't you?

Ken: Yes, I do understand there's a difference, but it's hard for me to figure out where my mind ends and I begin.

PB: That is very well put. Meditation can help you with that. While there is no one right way to meditate, it's important to put yourself in

The Power of Self Awareness

a meditative situation as often as reasonably possible. This may mean finding regular time alone when you can just close your eyes and sit quietly, even for a brief period. You can begin simply by observing your breathing. The more you do this, the more you will begin to separate from the busyness of the mind. As you focus on the rise and fall of your abdomen or on the air going in and out of your nose, your mind will slow down and your body will become relaxed.

Ken: What do you think about when you meditate? Or do you try not to think of anything?

PB: I begin, as I said, by watching my breath. As you observe your breath, you will find it slows down without any effort on your part, and your heartbeat slows as well. Breathing is from the autonomic system, so it happens without your having to think about it. This points to the fact that our life is not our own—we are being *breathed through*. The heart beats from the autonomic system too, so we are not in charge of our heartbeat either. The more you consider all of this, the more you'll know you are not your body and you are not in charge of your body.

Meditation is akin to self-hypnosis because you can mentally tell yourself to go into a deeper, more meditative state of mind and you'll go

Ken's Story

there. Once you are in that state, you enter a different level of consciousness and experience greater spiritual awareness. For example, you can call your father in from the spirit world and talk to him. Especially if you meditate regularly, he will be aware of the opportunity and he'll come. This doesn't mean that in the beginning you will clearly see or hear your father, but if you work with this in meditation and passively watch and listen, you will become increasingly able to communicate with him.

Also in meditation, you may simply want to detach from your daily life and enter a sphere of peace, or a "do-nothing" state, and some appreciate using a mantra for this purpose. For years I used the words, "So calm" to help me enter a meditative state, and I still recommend it to students. Every time you breathe in, you can silently say the word "so" and when you breathe out you can say "calm." Words ending in the letters "m" or "n" create a vibration that brings the right and left hemispheres of the brain into oneness.

True meditation takes place when the two halves of the brain are without conflict or separation. Great peace comes when that happens. That's why the word "om" works, and I use it as well, because it also creates a vibration between the two brain hemispheres that brings them into harmony. Sometimes I use a more advanced mantra, "I am."

Ken: Why is that more advanced?

PB: Because "I am" is the statement of highest being—the expression of a state of non-attachment. It doesn't say "I am this" or "I am that" but just says, "I am." It's another way of saying, "I am being." Think of these words as a doorway between heaven and earth. If you say, "I am a teacher, I am on earth, I am a person who earns 'x' amount of money or likes to eat 'y' kind of food, I am afraid, I am happy," you are expressing attachment to earthly things. But if you say, "I am spirit, I am an eternal being, I am filled with eternal joy and peace, I am one with God, I am God, I am not different from God," you move in the direction of a very different awareness. Just saying the words, "I am" will help you experience this.

People usually identify more with earthly than spiritual things, but whether we know it or not, we are eternal beings. Ultimately, we spend only a short time on earth, and the purpose of earthly life is to prepare for life in the spirit world. If we live as though physical life is the

Ken's Story

beginning, middle, and end of all life, the spirit may have problems making the transition into the spirit world and be drawn back to earthly attachments. This doesn't mean that one should become a monk or go into a cave and live apart from the world. It just means to be aware of what one becomes attached to.

When you say the words, "I am," you are not saying anything about the earthly realm or the spiritual realm—just about pure being, without regard to being involved with either sphere. It's what you *are* essentially in the state of highest purity. Do you understand?

Ken: Yes. It's just accepting the fact that you *are*.

PB: Yes. Saying the words "I am" puts you in touch with your true nature. These words open a door that swings both ways—toward earth or toward spirit. The more you use them in meditation, the more detached you become from the earth plane, and that's the secret of gaining personal self-mastery. The simpler your approach to meditation, the faster you will gain dominance over the mind. It's not an esoteric or complicated idea.

My advice is to start out by focusing on your breath and do that for a while before moving on to something else. You will find yourself beginning to observe your mind, and you'll actually experience that you are not your mind but separate from your mind. You'll see that you're the one watching and your mind is being watched. If you were your mind, you couldn't watch it, could you?

Ken: No.

PB: The eye can't see itself.

Ken: I like that.

PB: The fact that you can look at your mind and watch your thoughts as they rise and fall, come and go, is the biggest clue that you are not your mind. Then who or what are you? Well, when you first come to earth, you're just "I am." But a child soon begins to notice things like hands and feet. When one of our grandchildren was very little, she looked at her hands and said with some amazement, "Oh, I have hands!" This was the beginning of her awakening to the fact that she is not her hands, her feet, or any part of her body.

Ken: She said that?

PB: Yes. And the more you dwell on being different from your mind, the more you will ask,

Ken's Story

"Well then, who or what am I?" That's a very good question to ask. In teaching about meditation and self-mastery, I always suggest that people ask the question, "Who am I?" The fact is that each of us is a divine, eternal spirit come to earth to occupy a body for a period of time, to go through whatever it is that we go through, and to enter the world of spirit again. You've already chosen to go through what you go through to learn all the lessons that you need or want to learn while you're on the earth plane. That's why it's important to always watch what's happening right in front of you, because that's where your life lessons always are.

Ken: Really...

PB: Yes. It's now, in these circumstances, and in this moment that the lessons of life exist. Right now, you're preoccupied with your father for a number of reasons. At some point ask yourself, through journaling or in meditation, "Why am I dwelling on my father and thinking about his presence? Why is all this happening?" Without thinking there is anything good or bad about it, just look at it and learn from it, because there is a lesson there. Once you've learned that lesson, you will move on to something else.

The Power of Self Awareness

The relationship with your father may go deeper, or as you become more mature, stable, self-confident, peaceful, and happy in yourself, he may come only periodically, and you may think of him only occasionally. This won't mean you don't love each other but that you've learned the lesson there is to learn from his closer presence. Does this make sense to you?

Ken: Yes, definitely. It helps a lot, because I haven't been detaching from all the things that happen around me. To hear there is a very clear distinction between my mind and what I am helps me to realize that not everything is as big a deal as I think it is, and not everything is as small a deal as I think it is.

PB: That is brilliant! I wish more people could understand as clearly and deeply as you have in saying those words. Yes—it's no big deal so I don't need to become attached; and yes—it *is* a big deal because there is an important lesson I need to learn. The longer you live, the more you realize that what's happening today is what you need to look at, but there's a good likelihood that in a few days it will be gone and something new will appear.

Ken: Right.

Ken's Story

PB: To sum up, we are not the mind, we are not the body, and we are not our thoughts or feelings. These are all means to engage with the earth plane. Meditation can lead to clairvoyance, clairaudience, clairsentience, and a high level of spiritual awareness that allows you to become peaceful and calm. Over time, it helps you develop greater ability to be accepting and objective in relation to people, events, experiences, thoughts, and feelings, all in the context of love for yourself and others. Those who apply these principles are successful in gaining dominion over their minds.

WORK AS A CLASSROOM

PB: You said you were concerned about your job. So what is the challenge there?

Ken: I enjoy teaching the kids, so that's not the problem. It's in timing each day to include doing the lesson plans, turning in documents, and answering fifty emails from my principal and other teachers. Also, I have really long hours: I wake up every morning at 5:00 AM, get home around 7:30 to 8:00 PM, and have a little more work to do in the evening. So from about 5:00 AM to 11:00 PM when I go to bed, I'm working straight through on things related to my job. I have been wondering if I'm wasting my time, but

The Power of Self Awareness

after talking with you, I realize that I'm doing all of this for some purpose, and there's something that I need to learn from all of this.

PB: Most of the lessons are about ourselves. That's what our life is about. It's not about our environment or other people. We can learn from people and our surroundings, but the most essential lessons are still about us. In your work situation, one of the positive things you're learning is that you have the ability to discipline yourself from 5:00 AM to 11:00 PM in order to do your job.

Ken: To be honest, that's one of the big lessons I need to learn. If I had jumped right into medical school or something like that, I would certainly have expected it to be tough to the point of being overwhelming; but here I am teaching, and I'm still pulling long hours and having a hard time getting everything done. If I can do this, I can probably do anything.

PB: Yes. It's important to understand that there are no mistakes in life, and I learned this the hard way. I finally woke up one day and said, "Hey, I'm not really in charge here." I try to be, but the things I want to do, I don't wind up doing, and vice versa. After working with thousands of

Ken's Story

people, I've learned that this is true for everyone. Seeing the truth of this is one of the clearest indications that there is a God. Though the presence of God may be very silent, the fact is that when we set out to do something, we often wind up doing something else. That's why we need to surrender to life—not to be resigned or passive, but to allow life to unfold.

Regarding all you have to do at work, I've heard from more than one new teacher about the arduous tasks of lesson planning and other administrative work, but I've also heard that it gets easier.

Ken: Yes, that's what I've heard as well.

PB: I've written my own lesson plans for the teaching that I do, so I have some idea about what your task is. The plans I prepared came out of my life experience and study, since I didn't have a guidebook or other teachers to consult. When I wrote my first lesson plans for teaching meditation and later for teaching people how to tune into and communicate with the spirit world, I found that I learned from doing the planning. I felt a lot of pressure because I was preparing to give out information that would affect lives if applied consistently, so I understand the pressure

The Power of Self Awareness

you're under. But it's like riding a bike; it will get easier, and you already know that.

Ken: Yes, I think it will.

PB: What do you love about your work?

Ken: To be honest, I haven't felt love for any aspect of my work, but I can see potential for that when I see the kids smile, or I say something that makes them smile. They trust me, and I'm with them throughout the course of the day when their parents aren't. I realize this is a big responsibility. They've been alive for seven years now, so by the end of this year, I will have been with them for an eighth of their lives. I like knowing that.

PB: Well, you have a great influence on them—more than you realize. I still remember my second, third, and fourth grade teachers. All my teachers were second parents to me, and I modeled myself after them more than they ever knew. You can be sure those little brains and hearts are just soaking up everything you are and everything you teach them. It's such a fortunate place to be, because you're responsible for shaping lives now and into eternity. In that sense, it's a sacred responsibility.

Ken's Story

From a spiritual point of view, the classroom is a temple, because the spirit guides and spiritual masters working with each pupil surround them in their school environment. Their guides and teachers are eager for them to get the best possible start in life; and of course, each child has a uniquely unfolding destiny. You can see how different each one is from the other. It's a wonderful setting for you and for them to learn many spiritual object lessons. I'm sure that you sometimes see yourself in them.

Ken: Yes.

PB: Can you say how?

Ken: Yes, definitely. There's one kid in the class who is super smart, but he doesn't talk a lot. Still, when he's looking at something or looking at you, you can almost see the wheels turning so quickly in his head. He reminds me of me when I was a kid and just thinking about everything all the time and finding answers more quickly than my classmates. Even with little things like lining up to go to the drinking fountain, he realizes that if he pretends not to pay attention, he can be the last person in the line and get the longest time to drink. That's the kind of stuff I did as a kid. He never really talks, but I know exactly what he's thinking and why he does certain things. I really enjoy watching him.

PB: You have him figured out.

Ken: Yes.

PB: Well it's a beautiful responsibility, and as you embrace the up and down side of it, you'll learn many things, including how to be a wonderful parent in the future.

Ken: I hope so.

PB: Well all the object lessons are there. You sometimes feel affection toward the children while you're working with them, don't you?

Ken: Oh, yes. I actually sometimes think about the kids I may have in the future.

PB: I would think so.

Ken: Yes. I visualize myself holding babies, holding my child's hand while walking down the sidewalk, or teaching him something. I don't know if that's normal, but I do it.

PB: I think it's natural. What we're saying is that one of the most valuable things about being a teacher of younger children is that you have the chance to learn lessons that ultimately teach

Ken's Story

you how to love. You know you can't just suddenly blow up in the room, even if you need to speak firmly to get a point across, and you know you can't reach out and slap a student when you're frustrated. You know the children are like sponges drinking up everything you put in front of them, though some are slower or quicker than others. Through all of these experiences, there are many lessons to help you become a wiser, more prepared parent and a more loving person generally.

I want to go back to a point I discussed before, the element of affection. Teaching is not only about giving out information but about giving out information in a loving way. And that's what endears teachers to children. I remember teachers whose teaching was good, but they showed no particular affection for us as they taught. By affection, I simply mean warmth, kindness, and understanding. The classroom is a great environment in which to learn love for all kinds of children and to convey that love as you teach. Aren't there some children you wish were not in your class?

Ken: To be honest, yes.

The Power of Self Awareness

PB: Of course. Every teacher has that experience. But again, these children have something to teach you—unconditional love.

Ken: Right. Each kid is like a mini-mission...

PB: I like that: "mini-mission."

While it's nothing new, I want to say something that deserves repeating many times: *It's not what happens to us in life that matters, but how we respond to what happens to us.* So here you are, having this experience of being a new teacher. Sometimes you dread going to work; sometimes you're tired, sometimes you wish you weren't in your job at all, and sometimes you find pleasure in it and feel a variety of positive feelings. The point I'm making is that it's not the job that's important but your attitude toward it. That's where all the important object lessons are in terms of self-mastery. Among other things, our conversation today will enable you to look at your attitude. You can allow it to evolve as you master your work and it flows more easily, becoming less like drudgery and bringing you more joy. As you gain more experience and skill, you will find yourself more and more secure about your work.

How many children do you have in your class?

Ken's Story

Ken: Right now there are twenty-six.

PB: That's a lot. Do you have an assistant?

Ken: Yes. I have a co-teacher.

PB: Well that's very fortunate. At least that person can pinch hit for you and take up the slack when needed. And do you have a good rapport with that teacher?

Ken: Yes, we have a good relationship.

PB: Is your co-teacher a man or woman?

Ken: A woman.

PB: Well that's a good balance. Older or younger than you?

Ken: She is a year older.

PB: Were you self-conscious in the beginning, teaching with her present?

Ken: No.

PB: That's very good.

EMBRACING OUR LIFE EXPERIENCE

PB: We can learn to embrace life as it unfolds, and this includes tragedies that sometimes come to all of us. You know this from coping with your father's death. You learned that you couldn't dwell in grief, sadness, or in missing him perpetually or neither of you could move on. From a practical and philosophical point of view, you learned how to embrace your father's death and find meaning in it—correct?

Ken: Yes. When I think of him now, I don't feel sad anymore. I know I'm going to see him again, and I'm one hundred percent sure of that. I think he's happier now, because he's in a good place, so I don't worry about him in that way. I'm not sad for me that I don't get to see him anymore. I just would like to talk to him, and that's really what I miss.

PB: Your father was an ultrasensitive man.

Ken: Yes. He was very sensitive.

PB: I didn't know him, but from working with you, I can imagine that he was very sensitive. If he had understood the metaphysical world better, he could have directed his spiritual gifts more intentionally. It would have helped him to know more about the dynamics of his own spirituality, including the kinds of things you and I are talking about today.

Ken: Yes. I kind of know what you're saying.

PB: Well, in the coming weeks, just see how this all plays out in your thinking.

If children were taught from the beginning that life is a series of object lessons, they would spend more time asking, "What is it I'm supposed to learn here?" They would spend more time really learning than in wasting time and energy by resisting reality as it unfolds.

Ken: Right.

Ken's Story

PB: You're fortunate because your mother was very purposeful, consistent, and loving, and she gave you a good beginning. You also have a philosophical character, and you look for deeper meaning in life. Many people are not like that, and you know this from those around you, don't you?

Ken: Yes; right.

PB: Tell me about it.

Ken: I can't talk about what I really want to talk about with most people because they think it's weird to talk about God or spirituality. But these are the things I'm most interested in and curious about.

PB: Well that's true for me, too. Through grade school and high school I wanted to talk about God; not about religion but about my spiritual experiences, because I had encounters with God and the spirit world from a very young age. It was hard to share this with anyone, so I felt very much alone inside. Like you, I got along with everyone because I was a positive person and had many leadership positions in my school. But inside, I had this hunger.

You are fortunate to have this as well, and it's no accident. You were born this way, and it is figuring greatly in who you are and who you

The Power of Self Awareness

are becoming. If you weren't aware of the element of spirituality in your life as much as you are, you'd be a very different person. Learning to master and direct this energy is the secret to becoming all that you can become.

Ken: That's my goal. When I was in college I was confused, and I just thought about what I could accomplish on a practical level during my life. But after reading your book, praying, talking with you, and thinking about what I really want, I am trying to be more connected to a spiritual direction.

PB: You're on the right path, and I want to confirm that. Because of your training, family upbringing, all the experiences you've had, and just being you, you're a more advanced soul than many at your age. And as long as you don't lose sight of it, you'll probably always be pursuing the higher life, the spiritual life, the inner life. This doesn't mean that you're not going to live out your life on earth in a realistic or practical way, but it's important to stay on the path of higher awareness.

I wish I had been able to talk to someone like this when I was young like you, as I think it would have changed my life. But I had to go through many object lessons in the school of hard knocks in order to become a teacher of spiritual subjects. In the end, everyone has to figure things out for themselves, even if they get good understanding from a teacher. I can be an authoritative teacher only because of my life lessons and not from gaining book knowledge or hearing about the truth from another person. That will be true for you, too. In fact, everyone must experience truth to really know it as their own.

You have had to go through many struggles, especially in losing your father as you did, but as you embrace everything positively, you'll find that you will be blessed by all of your life experiences. It's when we try to run away from pain or the reality of our own shortcomings that they follow us. When you turn around and just look at reality, whatever it is, and embrace it, the pain begins to go away. It is ultimately replaced by understanding that leads to compassion for yourself and others. If you live according to this understanding, you will learn life's deepest object lessons. Does that make sense?

Ken: Yes, it makes perfect sense.

PB: Just the fact that you're asking to talk about the deeper things of life, particularly spiritual things, reflects very well on your philosophy and the direction you are moving in.

The Power of Self Awareness

Ken: Thank you.

PB: Well you'll be a helper to many other people. Whether you become a doctor or remain a teacher, you'll still find yourself drawn to spiritual things, and you may even become involved in teaching other people what you've learned. The most important student to teach, however, is yourself; and if you learn well, even if you don't teach anyone else, that's enough.

Sometimes we think we have to save other people, but the God that lives in me lives in you, and God is just as involved in your life as in my life. Because I have that awareness in relation to my children, I don't worry about them. They may not walk the path I walk or do things as I would, but they have to live their lives, and I deeply respect that. I'm able to feel secure in watching them find their own way because I'm highly aware that the spiritual cause of life is guiding them. I know they will learn from life as I did—that life itself will teach them. Often I think that our experience is the greatest manifestation of God, because life *is* God. And since life teaches us, we can also say that God teaches us through life. So we learn. I see it all the time in myself and in others, and it's the same for you.

WE ALL HAVE TRUTH

Ken: We're lucky to have you.

PB: Well, I appreciate that. But the important thing to know is that we all have truth. Even as a child, I used to think there was a certain place within me that I called a "truth box," and I somehow knew that if I went inside I could find the answer to anything. I would go inside and just ponder and ponder and ponder. I think my mentality was more Eastern than Western because I sought to solve problems not by arguing or fighting but by thinking things through and trying to understand.

Ken: Is that the Eastern way?

The Power of Self Awareness

PB: Yes. It's at least generally true that Western culture has been progressive in external things, and Eastern culture has been progressive in understanding the inner life. The contemplative state is more familiar to those in the Far East because it is more central in their religious teachings, including going inside to meditate and become more aware of the inner self. But this spiritual approach has been brought to the West by various teachers, and it is gaining ground here.

Ken: I think that's good.

PB: In what ways do you see yourself as different from or the same as other people?

Ken: I guess it would depend on the person I'm comparing myself to.

PB: Good answer.

Ken: I find out a lot about who I am in the way that I want to take care of my body. I take pride in being healthy and keeping myself strong and fit, so I tend to respect what others do to take care of their bodies. For me, my body is a great tool that should be taken care of. I do find that I'm different from many people in that respect, especially here in America.

Ken's Story

In my attitude about other things, I usually have no strong opinions, and I'm non-competitive about ideas. For example, I was talking with a friend several months ago who was telling me about a problem he was having with his parents. He told me why he was upset and why they were upset, but he was obviously speaking from his own point of view. Even though he was a good friend, I immediately recognized that I couldn't side with him because I realized he wasn't seeing his situation objectively. Because I didn't have all of the information from all points of view, I couldn't decide whose side I was on.

Long story short, when there's a problem, I see each side so clearly that I can relate to where all the parties are coming from. I think that differentiates me from many people who are more opinionated. I've seen that it's hard for people to change their minds once they have something in their heads, and they become kind of blind to any other viewpoint.

PB: Well, you have a gift. At your age—or at any age—it's a valuable trait to be able to retain objectivity and seek the truth of things instead of jumping to conclusions. An opinion might be the truth, but sometimes it is just a personal point of view, as you say. It's always important to try to find the truth.

I think you're also the kind of person who makes friends easily.

Ken: Oh, yes. I really have no enemies. When I meet someone, I don't say I do or don't like the person. I make friends very, very easily, and I feel fortunate to be like that, I guess.

PB: Yes. This makes you a universal kind of person who can lead others. The first and most important lesson to learn in life is to love all people everywhere as yourself. This is possible when you have no stories about what kind of individual you do or don't like, or what kind of person you are meeting. Instead, you accept people where and as they are. The only true story is that everyone else, at the core, is like oneself.

Ken: That's very true.

PB: We are all from the same origin, though we may manifest in different bodies and minds. Our essence is the same, and God is present in everyone. Divine intelligence and divine love are present in everyone, and that's our common ground. This doesn't mean we don't exercise discernment in choosing who to spend time with, but it does allow us to love all kinds of people.

Ken's Story

We may each have a different path, but we are all on the same mountain of life, aren't we?

Ken: Yes, absolutely.

PB: And all of our paths lead to the same place—the top. Once we arrive there, we find out, "Oh, we may have been climbing on different paths, but we have all been on the same mountain, reaching for the same goal." That goal is the awakening to our individual and shared God-presence, but that's an overarching goal that most people don't realize early or even late in life. Many realize it only when they pass over into the spirit world. Then they understand, "Oh, I should have been paying attention differently. I should have been looking at my own path, not someone else's path. I should have been looking up, not down. I should have listened more than I talked. I should have spent more time going inside rather than focusing on external things."

Beyond you and me as personalities, what's important is the truth we're discussing because that's what sets us free. It may be a cliché to say that, but it's true! It's only if we look at the truth in our lives that we develop real understanding.

SAINT GERMAIN
AND SPIRIT GUIDES

PB: Is there anything else you want to ask?

Ken: For some reason, I keep thinking of Saint Germain.[2] So the next time you speak with him, please tell him I said hello.

PB: I'm sure he's very touched by that.

Ken: Yes. I was thinking about him last night, actually.

PB: Oh, really? In what context?

Ken: I don't know. When I was reading one of your books a couple of years ago, you described

---

[2] Saint Germain is a spiritual master in the spirit world who is also Philip's master guide.

The Power of Self Awareness

what he looked like when you first saw him, with purple light surrounding him. Sometimes I think of a figure in purple, and it makes me think of Saint Germain. That's how he'll pop into my head once in a while.

PB: Well if you think of unconditional love, then that's Saint Germain. He's a great master of that. The fact that you periodically think of him probably means he's with you.

Ken: Really?

PB: Yes. I don't want to make people self-conscious about this point, but I'm aware that a large percentage of people who come to me are being shepherded by Saint Germain, because he's like an over soul. People have their own immediate master teachers and guides, but the overall master for many people I meet is Saint Germain. I want people to identify with their own teachers first, but it's true that Saint Germain is working very hard to bring like-minded people together—those who understand the higher levels of spirituality, particularly that God lives within us and that the light God is, we are. Saint Germain is seeking to help people understand and master this reality.

So when you think of him, just know he's really there.

Ken's Story

Ken: Okay. So you don't think I'm imagining all of this because I read about him in your books?

PB: It can be a combination of factors, and certainly imagination can play a role, but I wouldn't analyze it too much. The forerunner and basis for any spirit's manifestation to us can be something that reminds us of them: a thought, a color, or a song. This kind of forethought is as important as the actual manifestation. Even if they aren't there immediately, as soon as we think of them, they come.

When we talk about our spirit teachers and guides, their role in relation to us is similar to your role in the classroom. In teaching children, you are overseeing and helping them master their lives in terms of academics and more. At the same time, if one of the children has a special need or problem and holds up a hand, you respond immediately, or you say, "I'll be with you in a few minutes." You're attentive to all the children as a group, but also to each individual. That's the way the spiritual masters are. The higher masters oversee many people, but as soon as one of the persons has a need, they become aware of them and go to them. And it isn't always just a need in the sense of there being a problem; they also visit out of affection.

The Power of Self Awareness

I sometimes feel Saint Germain around me just because he loves me and I love him. There doesn't need to be a profound reason. In the beginning, Saint Germain spoke to me out loud, and I have it recorded. He said, "You are being held within my hand, and you can't go wrong. And you have to know that." And then he said, "When I say you're being held within my hand, I'm saying I love you, and in love, we never give up. We never condemn."

So if any of the masters come and spend time with you, their most essential reason is love. They care about you as an individual soul, because they know your destiny. They're helping you walk the path to fulfill the various things that you're intended to fulfill, and they have a clear map of where you are going, even if you don't. Does that make sense to you?

Ken: Yes, definitely.

WHERE TO FROM HERE?

PB: Is there anything else you want to talk about?

Ken: Well, when I spoke with you the last time, I felt that in return for all the help you have given me and others, I wanted to do something to help too. I know I'm young and not very knowledgeable, but if there's ever anything I can help you with, I want you to know I'd be happy to do that.

PB: Well, that's kind of you, and I appreciate what you said very much. I feel rich because I get a chance to share many lives, including the deepest parts of them. As a medium, I am used for this purpose over and over. Some of the words that come out of my mouth I have never

The Power of Self Awareness

heard before, and I benefit from that, too, so it's a win-win situation.

Being in this kind of work has great rewards, but you have to stay aligned with the spiritual presence that is working with you, whether it's Saint Germain or almighty God. And since every day is new, you have to participate in that partnership consciously. Probably the single most important thing I do is to try to stay aligned with the guidance of spirit, and this requires returning again and again to my central purpose. It's a blessing, inasmuch as there are many rewards that come from walking the spiritual path, but it requires much discipline to stay on course.

Now, let's begin to sum up this conversation. If you would, please close your eyes for a moment and try to feel whatever it is you're feeling in your heart and in your being. Tell me if you're feeling any different from when we began talking.

Ken: I feel a little more complete. As I visualize the inside of my body, I can see a space, and it feels solid. On the journey in front of me, I feel as though things are going to happen, and whether these things are in or out of my control, I just have to live. In relation to my dad, I know he'll be there for me, but I need to work

Ken's Story

at meditating and calling him in. It's so good to know that he's happy.

PB: The wonderful thing is that we haven't said anything that's extremely profound or esoteric. We're speaking a common language to share simple truths. But the more we contemplate all that we've talked about in terms of the spiritual path, Self-realization, and God-realization, the more peace comes over us, and the richer we feel. This is because these are the highest and most important truths for our lives on earth and our eternal existence. When people are open enough to really take them in, this makes a huge qualitative difference in their lives. Can you feel that?

Ken: Yes.

PB: Because of the truth in our conversation, it will echo not just for days or hours but for years of your life. The information we're discussing is eternal in nature and centrally important to each of us.

Recently, a medium told me that he had the feeling that I was anxious about my work because I have so much to do and so little time to do it. If I'm anxious about anything, it's about wanting to help more people on earth to realize who they are and understand more about the spiritual realities of life. Most people don't become concerned about these things until their later years.

Ken: Even though I'm young, I'm starting to become more aware, and I had a good upbringing as far as spirituality goes.

PB: Yes. You are very fortunate. Continue to love being you, and do not want to be anyone else or anywhere different from who and where you are. That's part of proper self-love. In a fundamental way, you are all that you have.

Ken: Right.

PB: Embrace each day and all of your days, and you will be doing yourself a great service. I grew up on a farm where we used to make butter. It didn't *look* like butter at first but like cream floating on top of milk. I don't know who found out that if you beat it for a while it will turn into butter. Well, that's like life. A newborn baby just coming out of the womb may not be very attractive, and it may look as lumpy as a baked potato. But the eyes of the mother can see only beauty because she is totally in love with her newborn. She sees all the great potential. People must parent themselves by embracing themselves as they

Ken's Story

are and seeing their own beauty and potential. Then they can turn from cream floating on the top of milk to butter.

Ken: I'll remember that...

PB: Yes. So just churn your life up until it turns to butter! [Laughter.]

Well, unless you have something else, I would like to close.

Ken: Yes.

PB: It will be most meaningful to me if you are able to use what we've talked about to enhance your experience by finding all of the precious gems in your life as you continue on your path toward your goals.

Ken: Yes; I will be keeping all of this in mind. Thank you.

PART II: FOLLOW UP CONVERSATION WITH KEN

BUILDING A SPIRITUAL LIFE

Ken: I've been doing a lot of thinking since we talked, and I can't stop thinking about the path I'm taking in life and wondering if I'm on the right track to end up where I want to be in the future. As I'm getting older, I'm appreciative of my youth and what I've accomplished so far, and I feel fortunate to have received such great gifts of mind, body, and spirit; but I always ask myself the same question: Am I truly happy doing what I'm doing now? And when I ask myself that, the answer is *no*. My first year of teaching in this national service program is almost over, but I signed a contract saying that I would teach for two years. There are no negative repercussions

The Power of Self Awareness

for me if I don't teach the second year, and I would like to move on and do something else, but I've given my word that I would do my best to stay and teach two years.

I remember two very important things from our last conversation: One was that some people go through life being unhappy with what they're doing instead of changing directions, and I am unhappy with what I'm doing, but another golden piece of information was that those who give up before they overcome an obstacle will face it in other ways until they overcome it. So—I'm torn as to what I should do.

THE HIGHER GOOD

PB: In situations where the results won't have long-term negative consequences for you or your work record, it may be okay to change directions in mid-stream. But it's also good to keep in mind that your resume will show that you taught only one year with this program, and you may be asked why you didn't continue. You just need to be ready to answer that question honestly in a way that reflects well on your judgment.

At this time in your life, however, one of the most important things you are doing is building your own character, and you raised this issue when you talked about your initial commitment to stay with this program for two years.

The Power of Self Awareness

So what's best for you not only in terms of your personal preference and work history but also in terms of your character? It's not only about my thoughts or emotions but about whether I'm being consistent toward the purpose of doing what's right in my own eyes. Following through is just one aspect of that.

From my experience and in talking to others, you would be most likely to make your grand breakthrough in your second year of teaching, so this decision is not really about anything in your external situation but about you. It's about being able to guide yourself to do what you don't feel like doing because it makes for real strength and a more advanced character—self-mastery. If it's emotionally challenging but not intolerable, that's one thing; but if it's so dangerous, stressful, or fatiguing that it's an undue hardship, that's another thing. Depending on how serious your discomfort is, you may want to ride it out and watch yourself change by embracing your work. If you do that, you can turn your experience into a building block of self-mastery.

How does what I'm saying sit with you?

GROWING THROUGH ADVERSITY

Ken: I think about all of this constantly, and I agree with what you're saying one hundred percent. Anyone can quit; but the people who stick it out grow. Knowing myself, I often think that if I did stop now and do something else, I would be immediately relieved and happy, but for the rest of my life, in the back of my head I would think I wasn't strong enough to fulfill my commitment.

PB: You would be facing the consequences of looking at yourself as doing less than what you thought was the higher path. In this case, leaving the program early wouldn't be so terrible; but

The Power of Self Awareness

we go from strength to strength when we follow through to discover depths of ourselves we can't find except by persisting through adversity for a good cause.

I'm in my twenty-seventh year of doing readings, and I've done thousands of them. To others it may look like a glorious career, but I don't really have any freedom. I always have to be on—to be sure I'm tuned up and tuned in. It's not easy to maintain the continual spiritual alignment that's required for my work, and I've wanted to quit many times. But when I look at what I feel in terms of my character, I'm very, very proud of what I've been able to do. I didn't give up, I didn't give in, and I kept on keeping on. I've tried to maintain this attitude toward everything I do.

There is nobility in maintaining consistency toward purpose, and if you are able to do that, your life can be an example you are proud to have others follow. When I was close to your age, I was in the army for three years, and I experienced extremely confrontational and even life-threatening situations. Because I embraced all of my experiences as my destiny, I got a lot out of my years in the army, even though I never wanted a military career. I would recommend the experience of national service to anyone,

Ken's Story

perhaps through something like the Peace Corps or the teaching program you are part of now. It's beneficial to all young men and women to serve others under conditions that challenge them. It teaches them the priceless lesson that they have more strength and a greater depth of character than they knew they had. It's only through facing our own weakness that we learn how strong we are.

EASIER IS NOT ALWAYS BETTER

PB: Too many role models for young Americans send a message that wealth, love, and prestige come cheaply, and that's a disservice to them. When celebrities, particularly rock and roll personalities, become popular enough, they set the standard for hairstyles, dress, attitude, language, and even behavior. But many of these "stars" fall quickly and far because they don't have the maturity to handle fame and fortune well. Some of them provide excellent examples by maintaining stable relationships and giving back to society, but too many get involved with drugs and alcohol and end up worse off than they

The Power of Self Awareness

might have been without their rise to fame. As we know, too many of them die young.

I gave a reading, several years ago, to a young woman who comes from a very prosperous family. She has enough money to last many lifetimes and doesn't really need to work. She wrote me a few months later to say how much she was helped by receiving a spiritual reading and reading some of my books. When I read for her, she asked the same question you are asking: *Should I continue with my current work or change my direction now?* Spirit gave the same answer I'm giving you today—that she should at least complete this phase of her work because of the opportunity it provides for building her character. She embraced this answer and is at peace with it. She knows she'll move on at some point, but she'll discover more of herself in the meantime. She wrote me that she is now having a good time with what she's doing. As you said before, if she had missed this opportunity to develop her character, she would have had to find it somewhere else.

You are investing in your character and not only your temporal future but your eternal future; for character is the only thing we possess and can take with us into the afterlife. Invest your energy and abilities in your job for as long

Ken's Story

as you are there, even if it's only for one more year. The more you invest, the more you'll get out of the experience. You're always interested in any activity, person, or thing you really invest in. So if you give your best to your work for as long as you are doing it, it's a win-win situation. You'll get the greatest benefit that way, and so will your students.

I'm glad you asked this question, though I'm sure I'm not telling you anything new. I just think it's important for you to look at it very objectively as you are doing today. How do you feel about what we've said thus far?

Ken: I feel good because the character-building aspect of it opens up a new perspective for me.

PB: Well there's a prize to be gained that you can't realize until you go through the whole two years.

Ken: Right.

PB: When you look back, you will perhaps have an *aha* moment when you say, "Ah, now I understand why I needed to keep on with this."

Ken: Yes.

THE SECOND TRUTH

PB: I know the neighborhood you're in is not safe. Is that a great concern for you?

Ken: I don't think twice about my physical safety. I actually feel safe all the time, and I'm never worried or scared. I think it has to do with the fact that while I was in college I started doing cheerleading, and as a result of that, I grew physically pretty strong. Then I decided to go into mixed martial arts and amateur fighting. This happened after my father died. I'm not sure why I did it, but it felt like the right thing to do at the time. The physical discipline I developed has helped me to become the person I am today, and

The Power of Self Awareness

I'm just more comfortable in my own skin. It's not that I would ever be violent toward anyone, but I do feel safe. It's hard to explain.

PB: Well, the body is the second truth. There are certain things we have to learn through living in the body, and as we master it, it imparts to our mind, heart, and soul, our *value*. The degree to which I really control my body in synch with my soul is the same degree to which I allow my soul or goodness to dominate my thoughts, emotions, and actions. There's a direct correlation. When we see someone who is very overweight, we know immediately that their soul message is not to do this to themselves, but still they do it. When this happens, their body is in control, not their higher consciousness. On the contrary, there is something really great about people who assume control to make their body what they want it to be and cause it to do what they want it to do. It's really not dissimilar from staying with a job when you don't like it—at least long enough to fulfill your obligation.

Ken: Right.

PB:. If a group of buildings is on fire and one of them is a bank containing your money, which one will you be most concerned about? Of course

Ken's Story

it will be the bank where you have invested your money and have your savings. The more you invest in a person, the more you come to understand and love that person, and it's the same with your job, self-care, physical discipline, and everything else.

By the way, I was a cheerleader for my last three years in high school, and it gave me a leading edge in my ability to work with myself that many of my contemporaries didn't have. It gave me self-confidence in many other areas too, because I had to do it before the public. As you know, I am still in the business of giving presentations before the public. If I wasn't good at cheerleading, I was going to get laughed off the floor, so I practiced enough to do it well. Being recognized as good at what I did also helped me to develop leadership skills.

Ken: Right.

PB: It has to do with having the courage to step out, even appearing as a fool sometimes, to bring home to yourself the messages that you are capable and you have value.

A SPIRITUAL CONNECTION

PB: Are you dating anyone now?

Ken: Yes. I met someone a few weeks ago, and we've been to dinner a few times. It's not serious though.

PB: My feeling is you don't really want a serious relationship right now.

Ken: I think you're picking up on the fact that I don't necessarily want a serious relationship with this particular person, but I would like a serious relationship. I'm very selective, though, and I think that to become serious, I would have to be one hundred percent attracted to the person

The Power of Self Awareness

mentally, spiritually, and physically. That's a hard thing to find.

PB: Are you of the mind that when the right person comes along, you'll know?

Ken: Yes, definitely.

PB: And do you think that person is being guided to you, even as we talk?

Ken: I'd like to think that. I hope that's the case.

PB: Well, there's a wide variety of explanations about how people meet, but sometimes it happens that people are not initially attracted to each other but grow into being attracted. Then there are times when people meet and really hit it off right away. It's case by case, according to particular personalities and the path of each person. I do think that you're the kind of person who wants a relationship that includes a spiritual connection.

Ken: Yes.

PB: What would that look like to you?

Ken: I want to be with someone who I could talk to about God and what I believe. When I meet people, I'm hesitant to express what I know about God and the spirit world, because many don't have beliefs similar to mine. I'm not

Ken's Story

embarrassed or ashamed of what I believe, but I know some people would not be comfortable with it because they don't understand it.

PB: Right. The other day I took my company logos to be framed by a fellow who has done other work for me, and while we were talking, I said, "I don't think I've ever told you that I'm a medium." He just lit up like a Christmas tree and said, "Oh, really?" I told him I was a channeler of Saint Germain, and he got even brighter. He used to be involved with others in this area who worked with Saint Germain's channeled writings. He and his wife also work with certain area mediums regularly, and they are both extremely interested in mediumship. We talked about the future of the world and many other things, and I realized that if I hadn't mentioned my work, I wouldn't have made this connection.

Obviously there are many times when I'm not moved to say anything about being a medium, so I think it's case by case. Just follow your intuition and common sense about what to share and when.

Is there anyone else around you would consider dating?

Ken: I keep myself open to meeting new people. The person I've been seeing lately is the roommate

The Power of Self Awareness

of a teacher I worked with, and she is also in the field of education. There is no one else I'm interested in right now.

PB: Well, you have plenty of time.

Ken: Yes. When I was in high school, I was only five feet three inches tall and weighed 180 pounds. So in my formative years, when everyone else was dating and flirting around, I just kind of kept to myself. Then, within one year, I shot up to become six feet two inches tall. Maybe because of my high school experience, I still have a humble approach to dating, and I'm happy for that. I'm lucky that I'm friendly and get along with most people. What I was like as a teenager slowed me down in my approach to women. I think that's good, and I don't think that happened by accident. It set me up to become the way I am with people now.

PB: How much do you weigh now?

Ken: Right now I'm at 190 pounds, and I lift weights every other day. Without bragging, I can say I'm in good shape. I'm actually trying to gain more weight. My goal is to be at 200 pounds. I think your body is the greatest gift you have on earth, and it's the gateway to controlling the physical world around you. You only get one, so treat it like gold.

THE DATING GAME

PB: That attitude would also make you want to treat your body as sacred when it comes to sharing it with someone through dating or marriage. You would want to know just who a person is and where they're coming from in terms of sex, love, philosophy, values, and commitment. Dating and marriage give you a lot to think about and a lot to take responsibility for. People draw to them what they are, so what you put out in this regard is what you get back. If you continue to hold proper self love, self direction, and self concern, you can't help but draw the right person toward you, and you can pray for that. Just put it out there.

The Power of Self Awareness

Today, people sometimes try each other out like they are trying out a car, and then they decide, no, this is not the car for me. It's difficult for young people because their hormones are designed to move them toward mating and procreation at a much younger age than they are economically or emotionally ready for in our society. They can either become very frustrated or go in the direction of having sex with many partners before they are financially and emotionally ready to marry. This can lead to confusion, regret, or even to a lifetime of being with the wrong mate. People need to use their heads as well as their hearts in making decisions in this area.

Ken: Yes.

PB: I admire the fact that you have self awareness about all of this, and it seems that you're pretty clear about what you want and don't want.

Ken: Yes. When I was growing up, my mother would always tell me, "You know, it's important to date different girls to figure out what you do and don't like." But when I was in my first year of college, I had never had a girlfriend or been in love before, and I met a very trusting girl and felt very, very strongly about her. Because she was

Ken's Story

the first girl I had dated, I didn't know if I would feel the same way with every girl or only with her. After eight months of dating, even though I was perfectly happy, I started feeling that I was too young to be so serious, but when I explained this to her, she was very upset. Nevertheless, we broke it off.

I still think about her to this day, even though I've dated a lot of girls since then. I've never felt anything close to what I felt with her. Looking back, I feel so fortunate to have been with her, because I truly believe that what I felt with her was genuine love. She taught me what it is to love someone.

PB: To care.

Ken: Yes, to care about someone—that's exactly it.

PB: Physically, emotionally and spiritually.

Ken: Yes. But it was still for the best that we broke up, because I was so young and just starting out in college. I'm just happy that I had the gift of knowing someone like her.

PB: Yes. So, what is your secret to disciplining yourself when it comes to sexuality?

The Power of Self Awareness

Ken: Well, if I were to sit here and say that I had a secret to disciplining myself, I wouldn't be completely honest, because I haven't been completely disciplined. In college, I went through a phase where I wasn't very close with my spirituality and didn't act in a way I'm proud of today. I got over that phase, and I realize that sex is not what it's all about.

PB: Well, if you evaluate your experience using religious teachings or beliefs, you might come up with one answer, but if you evaluate it in terms of life experience you'd come up with another. Life teaches us, and because I work with so many people, I know that people go through all kinds of things and learn from them. So from my perspective, I don't see sexual experience as right or wrong. I'm not saying this to mean we should just throw everything to the wind and do whatever we feel like doing, but I think it's best to deal with our sexual behavior in a very realistic way. If we over-indulge to the extent we get lost in a hyper-sexual lifestyle, we will lose track of the higher reality we're all ultimately headed toward, which is self-mastery.

Some of the higher beings we call spiritual masters went through similar things. We call them masters because they eventually mastered themselves, including their own bodies and their own behaviors. They gradually put everything into proper perspective, weighing the value of one thing against another and looking at the long-term and short-term outcomes of their actions. They made conscious decisions such as, "This I will do," and "This I won't do," but their decisions didn't come easily. They had to gain perspective through experience and self-understanding to develop their own philosophy and attitude. I think you know exactly what I'm talking about.

Ken: Absolutely; definitely.

PB: Did working with martial arts and other physical disciplines help you to see the sexual area of your life more clearly?

Ken: I think so. When I was younger and out on my own for the first time, I was not making such good decisions and I was partying a lot. But when I started working out and doing sports, I realized I had to choose between the well-being and maintenance of my body and its destruction through too much partying. Once I was maintaining my body and taking care of it, I wasn't in situations where I was making bad decisions. The sports and physical work I did absolutely helped me to maintain more self discipline.

TRANSFORMING ENERGY

PB: Well, as I often say, you can't create energy and you can't destroy it; you can only transform it. When you understand that principle, you know that sexual energy is like all energy; it's just there. It's not inert but active, and it pushes us toward procreation or the expression of love—to me they're the same thing. When we understand this, we can sublimate sexual energy or transform it by bringing it to a different level. Many spiritual masters, especially in India, learn how to raise sexual energy from the base of the spine to the brain where it is transformed into spiritual awareness that's far beyond sexual

The Power of Self Awareness

ecstasy. They are able to transform their physical energy into spiritual energy because the essence of all energy is spiritual.

Ken: Yes.

PB: I always ask myself if I am struggling with another person, myself, my body or whatever, "Ok, what else can I do with this energy?" I can either enter into it in a negative way or transform it into something positive through my creative and conscious effort. My usual response to conflict with people is to either stop interacting with them—though not in a confrontational way—or just come back to them with a lot of love and positivity. I don't want to hurt myself or anyone else, so I seek to transform negative energy into higher more positive energy. It's a challenge, but I think it's an art form in the area of relationships. It's a different version and degree of what we were talking about—transforming energy by raising the kundalini energy up to the crown chakra for the purpose of pure and total enlightenment.

Ken: Now that you've mentioned the chakras, I think I know what you're talking about.

PB: Yes. Sexual energy manifests on the two bottom chakras—the creative chakras. Great leaders usually do have great sexual energy, but to be successful in their spiritual aspirations, they transform that energy into higher expression. Some don't, and you have heard about spiritual teachers who have allegedly been sexually involved with their followers in an inappropriate way. This can happen to those who lose their objective awareness and get caught up in their physical reality.

Thousands of years ago, St. Paul said that he who sins is a slave to sin. I don't use the word sin in my work because it means different things to different people, but Paul's point is that if we are driven by our appetite for physical pleasure or power, we get trapped to the point that we become slaves to these things. And I think it's a great part of the reason there is so much dark energy in the world today.

Young people get involved with behaviors that harm them because of group influence, the desire to conform, or fit in, and the fear of not being liked. Once they go in that direction, they lose themselves. To follow what they think they see in the life of the latest cultural idol in music or movies, they may adopt cynical attitudes and drink, do drugs, or have indiscriminate sex. Through study, talking to people, and using common sense, some young people are able

The Power of Self Awareness

to take the same energy that is squandered in negative activities and instead direct it toward constructive ends—including service, proper self-love, and divinity. And the reward for doing that is great: It's the ever-expanding experience of becoming one with God.

Ken: Right.

PB: I do not intend to place sexuality in a negative frame. It's just important to know that how you use sexuality determines its value. I think you know that already.

Ken: Right. That's more than interesting.

PB: Well, you can be a Buddha or you can be a brute! [Laughter] Buddha is one who decided to leave all the physical pleasures behind. He did marry and have a son but left everything to pursue his spiritual destiny. I think he was called to do that, but I don't think that's the way for every man to be. After searching and searching, Buddha found Nirvana. He entered into his highest self and realized, using different words, that he was God or God was within him. You can't discover such a reality within yourself without heading toward it consciously. Some may encounter it by accident, but to maintain the

Ken's Story

awareness you have to become conscious of it. That's what the Far Eastern or Indian spiritual masters did.

Ken: Am I right to think that Buddha was a very real person?

PB: Well, there's a great deal of myth surrounding him, even as there is with Jesus and others, but the core teachings are true, and I've met Buddha in spirit. Just before I went to Japan for two months to do spiritual readings, I was sitting on the floor in my totally darkened meditation room contemplating and praying, when all of a sudden a golden glow began to form about four feet away from me over my prayer altar. Out of it Buddha appeared in full, glorious form, and I knew immediately that he came because of my forthcoming trip. He spoke in an audible voice saying, "Don't worry about Japan; I will be with you, and I will help you. You will do well." With that he faded from my sight, leaving a heavenly energy of profound peace and love permeating the room and my whole being.

One of the first people I read for in Japan was a beautiful elderly woman who walked in with an air of heavenly nobility. She took my breath away with her presence. After a few short exchanges, I said a short prayer and began tuning in to her spiritual energies and Jesus appeared directly behind her in a long white robe tied simply at the waist with a matching white belt. To say that I was surprised is an understatement! I thought to myself, "Philip! This is Japan. Buddha should be standing there, not Jesus!" But I never pull punches or make anything up, so I told her exactly what I saw.

Ken: Did you have a translator?

PB: Yes. But the woman spoke very good English, and I said, "I don't understand this, but Jesus is appearing behind you." She started crying, and said, "Well I'm a Christian, and I just feel so unworthy to have Jesus appear. For him to come like this means so much to me." To say the least, it was a profound moment and a lesson learned for me.

Buddha also appeared a number of times with other clients while I was in Japan. Whenever I do readings for people with whom Buddha works, he comes in just as clear as a bell. Sometimes Jesus and Buddha will appear simultaneously, or one will come before the other, and I'll tell the person that I can see that they are somehow positioned between the religious or spiritual thought of the East and the West. They'll often respond that they studied Eastern religion but have a Christian heritage or something like that.

Ken: Wow . . .

MAINTAINING BALANCE

PB: Well, I've digressed here, and we've come far afield from where we first began talking, Ken. So, are we answering your questions well, or is there something else you want to talk about?

Ken: Well, we've talked about my main concern.

PB: About staying the course with your teaching job for now?

Ken: Right. And I think we've addressed that very well. But my other question is, "How are *you* doing?" [Laughter.] I know you said your back was bothering you.

The Power of Self Awareness

PB: Well, talking this way brings a lot of high spirit around me, and the energy they bring is very healing. My back is not nearly as bad as it was when you first called. I've noticed very positive energy, like golden light, coming in as we've been talking, so it's better. Thank you for asking.

I'm anxious to get on with my teleconference classes, and I hope you have time to take some of them. If you can't attend the live teleconferences, the recorded class will eventually be available on my website where you can go into my online store and purchase them, download them, and listen to them on your own. The classes are all about the topics we've talked about and more. I don't have an expectation that you should take them, but they could be meaningful to you in advancing your appreciation of yourself and your ability to use your energies to become more aware of your inner gifts. One of the hardest things you will be learning in future years is how to strike a balance between being a spiritual person and using your spiritual awareness to deal with the practical realities of living on earth.

Ken: Yes. I know it will be hard because it's not always easy to see where one ends and the other begins.

Ken's Story

PB: Expand on that point.

Ken: Well, you know, I'm just figuring out how much of what I'm feeling and doing is based on earthly needs or things that matter strictly in the physical realm, and how much is based on the realities of the spiritual realm.

PB: I understand. So for me and people like me, the biggest question is, "How do I strike a balance between being a human being on earth and being someone who is ardently seeking to become one with God?" Can the two directions be reconciled? Yes, they can. It's just a matter of how. Some spiritual teachers in India and the Far East have the idea that to really be one with God you need to be single and totally devoted to that ideal. Others say you're in a body so you need to experience this life as a means to the end of discovering your own divinity and God within yourself, your wife, your children, and others. These are two distinctly different schools of thought, and I embrace the latter.

In India, at about the age of sixty, husbands and wives remain together but may deliberately begin to prepare themselves for passing into the spirit world. Their guru or teacher may tell them to begin spending much time in meditation in preparation to go over at the highest level of existence in the spirit world. The ideal is to come into the very presence of God in the highest of highest realms.

Have you read Yogananda's book, *Autobiography of a Yogi*?

Ken: No.

PB: My inclination is to tell you to read it because it will help you find yourself and put your life into spiritual perspective. It's the story of Yogananda's inner life and spiritual attainment as well as his experiences from his childhood in India through his time in America as a spiritual teacher. It is one of the greatest and most widely-read autobiographies about a spiritual teacher's life.

Ken: Interesting.

PB: A teacher in Yogananda's spiritual lineage—his own guru's teacher, Lahiri Mahasaya—was married, had children, and lived as a householder (working in an office) while he lived a very devoted spiritual life. His purpose was to teach others what he knew. His wife was less devout, but one night she woke up to find him levitating—floating over their bed.

Ken: Really...

Ken's Story

PB: You'll read about it in Yogananda's book. When Mahasaya's wife realized who her husband really was, from that time on she became his devoted disciple.

I was initiated into Kriya Yoga meditation by his great-grandson Shibendu Lahiri a couple of years ago. In any case, I have also felt called to devote my life to helping others understand and appreciate their own spirituality, but it hasn't taken me away from my marriage, my children, or my grandchildren. They're all part and parcel of who I am, and I wouldn't want any of them out of my life. But serving others through the truth that I know—specifically to help others understand their spirituality and become one with God—has become my core drive. It's the highest purpose I could devote myself to, and I believe I was called to it.

Ken: As always, I feel so fortunate and grateful that you have taken so much time to talk to me. I appreciate every minute of it. It's hard to find people with whom I can talk like this, including the frustrations I'm feeling. I honestly feel blessed to have someone like you in my life to help me think about things.

PB: Well, thank you. My major concern is that you go away from this conversation with a clearer sense of where you are, what you're committed to, and how you will carry out your commitment. The spiritual part of our conversation is important, particularly for a person like you, but use our discussion to also consider your physical wellbeing, your everyday tasks, and your career decisions. It was an honor to talk with you. God bless you.

May I close with a prayer?

Ken: Yes, please.

PB: *Our dear Father, we call you "Father" because we feel your parental concern and personal love. And if there is anything that you are, it's love. As Saint Germain said, in love we never give up and we never condemn. Most of all, we need to apply this to ourselves: to never give up on ourselves and to never condemn ourselves, but to always accept ourselves as we are, for who we are and where we are, and go from there.*

Please guide Ken in every part of his life and lead him to know that you are ever-present, whether he's aware of you or not. You are the presence of goodness, laughter, and all that is loving in human beings. You're also present in the sun, the moon, and in every part of nature—both the wild and peaceful aspects. Your wisdom is ever guiding us to the right outcomes in our lives.

Ken's Story

Be within Ken making all of his choices, and may he find the peace that he already is inside through meditation, reflection, contemplation, and just being. Help him to live in peace perpetually and work from that point outward. Give him a growing awareness of you and how you manifest in his life.

Thank you for this conversation and for the opportunity to share about all the lessons of life we can learn. Thank you for creating life so that we can be part of it and find all the treasures you have prepared for us. I pray and ask all of this in divine love. Amen.

Mastery Press

Phoenix, Arizona

For general inquiries send an email to
PB@PhilipBurley.com, or write to:

Adventures in Mastery, LLC (AIM)
P.O. Box 43548
Phoenix, AZ 85080

For more information about Philip Burley
and the work of
Adventures in Mastery, LLC,
please visit this website:
www.PhilipBurley.com

CPSIA information can be obtained
at www.ICGtesting.com
Printed in the USA
LVHW091046101119
636874LV00001B/377/P